Claver Lukoki
07562 203 735
purposeofexistence@hotmail.com

Published by Greater Works Publishing
United Kingdom
unlikelychampion@gmail.com
WhatsApp number: 44 7770 027557

ENDORSEMENT

The compelling fact of Claver Lukoki's life is that he carries a burning passion to impact, envision and influence his generation to rise to their God intended purpose and to make a difference in their own lives and their generation. His book contains great revelation knowledge. If you are not sure of your life's worth and purpose, I highly recommend this book to you.

Bishop Abel Kungu Snr.
President & Apostolic Leader of Acts of Faith Ministries International & Acts of Faith Ministerial Association (AFMA) Bedford, United Kingdom.

THE PURPOSE OF EXISTENCE II: THE REDEMPTIVE PATH

CLAVER LUKOKI

WORDS FOR THE NEXT GENERATION

Purpose was something I thought was an achievement you learn further down the line in life as you grow up. However, I have learnt that it can start right now and can only be done with God's help. Moreover, I have learnt that planning what I want to do further on in life is difficult in a world of 24/7 access to information. So, getting a head start with Claver has been hugely beneficial and I am learning more about myself as well every day.
— *Janeil*

I used to think that you had to be an adult to discover your purpose, but now, I know it can be done at any age with the help of the Lord. This is only the start, and Claver has helped me with it. To be honest, I would have never thought of doing this, but I am lucky to have Claver. This is only the beginning.
— *Abel Kungu Jnr*

I always thought that purpose was for adults, and I'm just a kid, so I'm not supposed to think about any of that. Now, Claver has taught me that it is best to know your purpose when you are young and to have a plan, so you know what to do in life. Your life revolves around your purpose and plan and if you do not know your purpose or have a plan, then what is the purpose of your life? If you were building a house, would you do it without a plan? If not, then why are you living your life without a plan. "A goal without a plan is just a dream" - Antoine de Saint-Exupéry. When I am older (or even now) I aspire to be an actress, but I cannot do that without a plan. This is not an easy job to get into, but I need to work hard. I am so blessed to have Claver in my life because without Him, I would not have discovered my purpose or had this opportunity so thank you. This is just the beginning of my life.

— *Tiaara Mpanumpanu*

Purpose. Something I had but did not see. Something I longed for but did not allow. I overlooked my purpose in a battle to figure out who I was & who I wanted to be. In a world with millions of people it would be silly to think you have to get through life alone without guidance or support from your loved ones. Asking for help can be hard; I have been there. However, being surrounded by people who are willing to help of the kindness of their own heart is rare. Claver not only took his time to help me understand the purpose of my existence, but many others alongside me too. I was already on my journey figuring out my purpose and was blessed with help along the way. I was a dreamer with no plans; I was filled with just hopes and dreams with no blueprint to follow.

Step by step, I began to understand the importance of a plan to reach my goals and live up to the expectations I had placed on myself. Writing a plan is easy following it and being motivated to achieve each step without skipping ones in between not so much, but day by day, I continue to work on it. Patience is something I lack I cannot lie but all good things take time. Life consists of battles we are unaware of ones that could easily throw you off track I would be lying if I said having a plan to look back on is not helpful in those unexpected times. God has a plan for me and with his guidance and the guidance of many more my purpose remains an open door ...

— *Anesu*

FOREWORD

Claver writes in such a way that will make you sit down and ponder on the journey of life. I am amazed at the way Claver draws attention to Christians living in a broken world full of distraction, fear, and at times, anxiety. There tends to be a consistent pattern that triggers our society from time to time, due to the pressure social media plays on us to 'look the part' and follow the path of influencers to be seen, to fit in, or to be chose— not realising that Christ already chose us when He died on the Cross. When you cannot find the answer, you tend to seek it through people, missing the voice of God because instant gratification feels much better than delayed hope.

The pain of leaving the earth without knowing what God has called us to do is not only heart-breaking, but a potential loss to the upcoming generation— allowing the voice of the world to be louder than the voice of God. Knowing who you are must be sought in the secret place (Psalm 91), and Claver has written this book to help lost souls find themselves in God.

Speaking from a transparent place, he understands how we feel and encourages us to wait on God to reveal His purpose. The aim for our existence is to live for God and please Him. We do not live to please people (Galatians 1:10), but to make disciples and be a blessing onto a nation blinded by the world's standards.

This book will enable you to walk in truth and not be burdened but cultivate a strong relationship with God to avoid being lost in a systematic society. Knowing the Father's freedom, this book will teach you how to find purpose, gain peace and find direction for your life. To all readers be intentional about finding out what God has called you to do. You are not here to exist but to leave an eternal legacy in the earth.

God richly bless you, Claver for your obedience to God in writing this book.

Esther Jacob
Entrepreneur, Author and Speaker

When Claver Lukoki asked me to write Him a foreword, I was truly honoured with the enlightenment he is trying to bring under the subject of purpose. It is inspirational to see a young man that is living according to his own purpose and want to help the nations to do same.

Our environment can shape our destiny and the big question is whether that destiny aligns with the assignment God has set us to complete on earth. The author stated that this is the most difficult phase of our life. At times, we do not find our purpose until our later stage in life, in addition, many deceased without fulfilling their purpose on earth.

It took Claver Lukoki some time for Him to find his purpose but eventually he did, which is the core motivation for Him to put his thoughts into literature. The inability of finding your purpose can lead to several factors such as insecurities, lack of fulfilment and satisfaction and you remain a spiritual orphan.

The book also touches the fact that many could be living a righteous life but still feel lost. This can lead them to seek alternative truths that could potentially not be the Lord's guidance.

Your purpose gives you a sense of direction and help; you complete your assignment on earth set by the Most High. However, with many distractions such as families, finances, careers, and other preoccupations that can really take us off our path of purpose.

Lack of results in your endeavours can also lead you astray and birth insecurities by witnessing others prosper with their endeavours. This book goes into details and illustrates different points why we could be lost while seeking for our purpose and how you can regain direction to pursue your original purpose on earth.

Napa Bafikele
Entrepreneur, Author and Speaker

ACKNOWLEDGEMENTS

First and foremost, I would like to thank my Lord Jesus Christ. In the process of putting this book together, I realised how privileged I am and how I have been favoured enough to write this book. Through the Holy Spirit, I have been enabled to have deeper insights and revelations of the Word and a knowing of my purpose. None of this would have been accomplished without my Father God. Therefore, I thank you Lord God for giving me the power to believe in my passion while pursuing my purpose and dreams. Without the Grace and the mercy of the Lord, I would not have been able to finalise this book.

To my father and mother, Kiyedi Lukombo and Kimbinga Mpembele Lukombo: I am truly blessed to call you my parents. I have come to the realisation that words are not enough to express my gratitude for all the wisdom, love, and support that you have given me. You are and have always been my number one fan and for that, I am eternally grateful. I pray that I will be a good parent to my children as you were and have always been to me.

To my brothers and sisters, I just want to say that I deeply love you all from the deepest depths of my heart. You all have always made me feel appreciated and loved. I am always amazed by your support, and I pray that this book will also help you to discover your ultimate purpose in Christ and live it out for the glory of God in Jesus Christ our Lord.

To my little brother Bradley and Nephew Omari: my only prayer for you both is that as you two grow older, that you will come into the knowledge of Christ Jesus and pursue Him alone for the rest of your life. I also pray that you two will know and fulfil your purpose to the LORD your God. Obey his directions, laws, commands, rules, and written instructions as they are recorded in His word. Then you will succeed in everything you do wherever you guys may go. I love you guys always.

My sincere thanks to my pastors, Bishop Abel, Success Kungu, Pastor Freddy, Lillian Maleka and Pastor Zorka Crichlow: I just want to say I am forever grateful and thankful for your continuous patience, love, and prayers. You all have given your lives to serve and to support individuals like myself. Thank you for believing in me and for the gift that has been bestowed upon by the Lord to glorify Him.

I thank the Next Generation Youths. Thank you for all your support and encouragement. You are the best and you have all motivated me to grow in my walk with the Lord and to become a better a leader. I pray that this book will also empower you to walk in your purpose.

To my fiancé, Rita Ndozi: Thank you very much for your love and constant support. You are the most amazing, wonderful, and beautiful woman I have ever met. You have no idea how happy you make me. Every day with you feels like a dream, but I know it is a reality. I am so blessed and thankful to the almighty God to have you in my life. There is nobody else I rather must fulfil my purpose with but with you alone. Thank you for loving me and thank you for making me feel so loved. I love you more than words can say. God knows. Thank you.

Finally, a big thank you to all my other family and friends. Although, I did not precisely mention your names, all your support and encouragement are invaluable.

TABLE OF CONTENTS

INTRODUCTION

Growing up is hard work. It is a part of life that pushes us to be our best selves, and yet, it can also leave us feeling significantly powerless and left behind. It is a rite of passage into adulthood, determining who you are and who you will become. It is about finding your purpose, and that is the most difficult part.

It is so easy to get caught up in life - we find ourselves pursuing careers based on the opinions of family and friends, or we pursue them because of our own interests and desires, but how often do we pursue a career because God told us? There are some people who find out very quickly the direction God wants them to take and embark on the journey incredibly early. Others find out much later in life, and some people go through their entire lives not knowing.

And for me, it took a little while to find out who I was.

My journey began a long time ago, and although I did not find my purpose straight away, there was an eventual breaking point in which God revealed my identity and purpose. Walking in that purpose, I was able to write my first book: *The Purpose of your Existence*, which is essential to read as it lays the foundation for this sequel.

With this book, I would like to draw into this concept even further in exploring the notion that you cannot be really fulfilled without first finding your purpose. When we do not find our purpose, we become lost, we become insecure and most importantly, we live our lives as orphans. This book will explore these points as well as how one may get on to a path of redemption if lost.

Now, in saying the word 'orphans', I am talking in a spiritual sense. A spiritual orphan does not know or understand the Father's heart, so they are always trying to please Him to get things from Him. This is very much like the prodigal son (Luke 15:11-32): although he had a good father, he kept on trying to perform and to please, and this is the worst thing that could ever happen to us as Christians.

Many of us are lost, even though we are walking with God. We are in church, and we are doing all the remarkable things that we are supposed to be doing. However, we are still lost spiritually. We still have not found the right path; we still have not come to the fullness of His truth; we still have not found our purpose - and most of the time, we are walking in alternative truths. Our perception of the truth does not meet up with reality. It is at this point that we need to begin our journey- a personal pursuit- of pursuing the Father for the truth. There are many things that can influence our journey along the way, which causes us to become lost and remain orphaned in our spiritual walk. This book endeavours to explain five of these key influences, and how you can work through them to remain on the path to finding your true purpose.

CHAPTER 1

SPIRITUAL BONDAGE

Let's talk about bondage. Yes, I mean tied up and restricted. It is bondage that holds us in a place where our spiritual vision is obstructed and stops us from hearing the Father's voice. There are many things in the spirit realm that bind our spiritual ears and eyes, and in doing so, it restricts our ability to receive the truth. So, what binds us from moving forward? What keeps us from knowing our purpose? A major part in this comes from the hurts of our past. It is important that we are healed from the things of the past— healed from the ancestral chains and bondage and healed from old mental theories and attitudes. It is particularly important that we allow God to deal with all those things inside of us. There are many things that I used to perceive a certain way but came to understand differently as I grew up and realised that my original perception had been wrong. For example, due to the rejection I had faced in my household and within my community, I grew up believing that if I did not have an identity, everyone would reject me. I had to receive deliverance from the bondage of rejection because it shaped my perceptions.

I completely rejected the concept of acceptance, and this made me withdraw even further from God. On the surface, it seemed as if I were walking with God; however, I could not accept the fact that God loved me or that I could even establish a relationship with Him. I suffered from this spirit of rejection, and I could not see that this was blocking me from fully experiencing Christ. It limited the truth in my life. There is no way I could have been one with God with all the bondage I had, which held my heart back from true relationship. I was seeking Him, but I was reserving a part of me for myself.

How could I fulfil any purpose with the spirit of rejection? All it was going to produce were more sinful ways and traps even whilst trying to do God's work. My work was being produced from a religious mindset.

Here on this earth, we are called for two main things: relationships and stewardship. We need intimacy with God for us to successfully steward what He has given us. At times, we tend to steward things without intimacy, but it is through an intimate relationship with God that we can do so most wisely and effectively. Therefore, God has been putting me on this path. Intimacy sets a higher standard than just having a relationship with Him. It is deeper; it requires giving my heart and my all to Him. Only He can measure if one is truly intimate with Him. Intimacy is about having total dependency on Him.

It was only when I went through a refining process with God, where He dealt with my identity, that I started to feel completely fulfilled in Him. The bondage that I faced did not allow me to experience the fullness of Christ. We tend to do things in a limited, half-hearted manner which prevents us from engaging deeper into God's will. It is our responsibility to discover our bondage so that we can deal with them and allow God to heal us.

FOR REFLECTION:

1. What do you sense the Lord saying to you from this chapter?

_____

_____

_____

2. Write down 3 scriptures you feel may apply to this chapter:

_____

_____

_____

3. As you reflect on this chapter, what step will you take in your journey with Christ?

_____

_____

_____

CHAPTER 2

FALSE IDENTITIES

In this chapter, we want to continue to talk about why people are lost. I am not talking about people who have never been saved; I am talking about people who are saved but are not walking in the fullness of the truth.

The Bible says in John 4:24, "For God is a spirit, so those who worship Him must worship Him in spirit and in truth."

God wants us to worship Him in truth, but what does that mean? It means that we should worship Him vulnerably with a full understanding of who we are in Him. David said, "Search me o God and know my heart, test me and know my anxious thoughts." Psalms 139:23

David's request here was for God to know everything about Him. He trusted God with his heart. We, too, must know His heart as well as know His ways. It is a huge responsibility. Vulnerability is a key part of growing in relationship with Him.

According to that scripture, living a life without a true identity that comes from God and not being aware of who you truly are does not allow you to deeply experience God. We tend to live out of false identities that have been formed from life experiences which makes us formulate a distorted perception of who God is.

Our identity can be shaped through our parents, schools, friends, and pastors. There are many things that have created this life that you have now and your perception of it. Many Christians are still walking with those false identities still ruling over them.

False identities created through 'our ways':

My family and I went to a certain church. We wanted to serve God, and we had a heart for God, but then we found this religion called 'Kimbanguism'. We were devoted members, but this had nothing to do with God. I believed that we went to this religion because of culture and tradition. We wanted God to deliver us, but we were approaching it in the wrong manner although our intentions were pure. Thank God, we came out of that! Over time, many family members have come into Christianity and have a fulfilling relationship and purpose in Jesus.

This is just an example to say that it is easy to walk in our own ways/cultures. The Bible says in 2 Chronicles 7: 14b "...and turn away from your wicked ways." What are our ways? Our ways or our cultures are patterns and behaviours that we have collected; things that we feel are our rights. Cultures are our family templates that we are immersed in since birth; culture is the way you live your day-to-day life. We feel it is our right to wake up late, do what we want to do or say whatever we want to say; we live out of entitlement. Even though those things in themselves do not seem bad in retrospect; however, these things may not be good for you. The Bible says, 'that not everything that is good is profitable for you' (1 Corinthians 10:23). It is these trivial things that prevent us from growing. The Bible says, 'little foxes spoil the vine' (Songs of Solomon 2:15). It is the same way with our idiosyncrasies and patterns of behaviour.

This means that you need the Spirit of God to decipher what is right for you and what is not right. Scripture says, 'If you walk in My ways and keep My instructions, then you will govern My house and will also have charge of My courts; and I will give you a place among these standing here (Zachariah 3:7)'.

This shows there is a difference between 'the ways of God' and 'our ways'. God wants to align us with His ways. In order to do so, God wants to deliver us from our cultures, traditions, mantras that we have created, theologies and theories that we have collected throughout life. We cannot do this unless we give up every tradition and culture. Now, do not get me wrong - some cultures and traditions are good because some of the principles that are rooted in the Bible. Nevertheless, some principles are not scriptural and are man-made.

And so, we need to reflect on those things that are holding us back. What are our truths? What is God's truth? Do we know the Father's heart enough to change ours? It is not easy to change a culture that has been ingrained in our entire selves, but it is a necessary step to being fully immersed in God's culture and finding our destiny.

FOR REFLECTION:

1. What do you sense the Lord saying to you from this chapter?

_____

_____

_____

2. Write down 3 scriptures you feel may apply to this chapter:

_____

_____

_____

3. As you reflect on this chapter, what step will you take in your journey with Christ?

_____

_____

_____

CHAPTER 3

RELIGIOUS THEOLOGIES

So far, I have talked about ways and cultures, but what about our religious theologies? Our religious background can create certain theologies in us. For example, I always believed that Jesus was white. Now, that is always up for debate, so I am not here to debate whether Jesus was white or black when He walked this earth. However, that is a concept I formed because of the way Jesus was portrayed in the church. This concept alone locked my mind to the possibility that Jesus could be a different race. This is a perfect example of how religion, as opposed to a true relationship with God, can limit us from accessing authentic encounters with Him. The idolatry of your theology is what hinders you from encountering the true person of Jesus.

Theology is the study of the nature of God and religious belief. What is your theology? Do you ever question this? It is important to address these misconceptions because they can limit our minds to who we think God is or what He is like.

Other things that I have believed include that Christianity was all about going to Heaven. I became focused on this, and I was believing it to be the single most important part of my walk with God. I had no other knowledge. I just believed that Christianity is all about Heaven and going to Heaven, and that was it. Due to that, I never came into any other knowledge until God started to reveal to me who He was. It was then that I began to understand that there is more to Christianity, God, and my spiritual journey than simply the destination.

Otherwise, all I was doing was just to please God out of legalism to make sure I was going to Heaven. However, the Father is a loving God. There is so much more to Him than I had thought at that time. He is calling us for intimacy and not religion. When this happens, He then gives us the keys to our destiny which gives us access to his palaces and kingdoms. He is the owner; He is the father of the universe; all silver and gold belong to Him (Haggai 2:8).

There are some things that we have learned over time and as a result, they have created a barrier between us and God. Perhaps, there are some experiences and encounters we will never come into simply because they do not line up with our theology. It is imperative to be aware of other perspectives and remain open to a change of theology—should the one we already adhere to be proven wrong. We need to be able to discern what to accept or not– this is what we need to be seeking.

In church, our focus should be on healing and developing the individual so that we have a healthy body of believers. When we are not working on individuals, then we are manufacturing a church that is lost. We see this happen repeatedly in our modern churches. For instance, in the Bible, every scripture has seven layers of truth to it. So, if we are not really pursuing truth to that depth, then people are not able to fully heal. Thus, the church will never grow and develop in the fullness faith. The pursuit of truth allows us to obtain deeper insight so that the church can reach its full stature in Christ.

Can you just imagine what He has in store for you? He has the key to your destiny, but He wants you to come into intimacy with Him. It is because He knows that when this happens, even if He gives you something that is so huge to handle, you will never turn away from Him because the relationship will keep you grounded. Most people have risen to stardom and become great in ministry, but many do not have deep intimacy with God. You find that the stardom takes them away from Jesus, as it has overtaken their spirituality even without realising it. I feel that in the old ages, God was doing things by grace, and He was lifting people, even without deep relationships. He was accelerating His ministers because He wanted His people saved; God wants His people to come into His kingdom.

However, in this new age, prophetically speaking, I feel that the dynamics in the spirit realm have changed. He is now bringing people into a relationship first and stewardship second. For us to succeed in stewardship, we need to let go of the theologies that are distracting us from a deep relationship and encounters with Him.

FOR REFLECTION:

1. What do you sense the Lord saying to you from this chapter?

_____

_____

_____

2. Write down 3 scriptures you feel may apply to this chapter:

_____

_____

_____

3. As you reflect on this chapter, what step will you take in your journey with Christ?

_____

_____

_____

CHAPTER 4

THE PURPOSE OF THE CHURCH

When we talk about our own purpose, we must also understand the purpose of the church, which is to train and equip individuals.

As the Bible says, God gave us five offices: The Apostles, the Prophets, the Evangelists, the Pastors, and Teachers. The church is called to equip us so that we can fully function in those offices (Ephesians 4:11-13). However, many of us are not equipped for our destinies, instead, we get philosophical knowledge without practicalities of the Kingdom.

For instance, we may be serving in church as an usher or an intercessor, which are important roles. However, if we are not progressing, then we may not have an impact in the Kingdom.

It is noticeable that even some leaders are not functioning in the correct identity, therefore, our churches are unable to function in the way that Christ desires.

When Jesus released the disciples into the world, He commissioned them to be productive and impact the world (Mathews 28: 19-20). However, our churches are not doing this. Other things are influencing the world on a larger scale, and this is a sign that we are lost and not in a healthy place with God.

So, what do we have to do?

In the next few chapters, I am going to talk about how you can stay on the redemptive path. We cannot control any situation, but we can take on some responsibilities that can change things for us. I will be talking about taking responsibility for our own healing, intimacy, identity, and stewardship.

These are the cultures of God. We must seek to walk in these cultures.

Why? It is because these cultures of God are the only thing that will transcend all the struggles. When we learn to be one with God, to walk in His ways and cultures, then it can conquer all these things that are derailing us from His ideal picture. This is what will ultimately heal our churches.

It is my cry that you can walk in that fullness of Christ and be free from every trace of lies or half-truths. It is my desire that we are fully immersed in who He is and realise that it is not about the routines, but that it is really about involving Him in all that you do.

FOR REFLECTION:

1. What do you sense the Lord saying to you from this chapter?

_____

_____

_____

2. Write down 3 scriptures you feel may apply to this chapter:

_____

_____

_____

3. As you reflect on this chapter, what step will you take in your journey with Christ?

_____

_____

_____

CHAPTER 5

TAKING RESPONSIBILITY

We must take responsibility for our destiny in Christ. We can be saved but remain lost because of all the reasons I have mentioned in our previous chapters. How can we and our churches stay on the right path?

Well, it takes a bit of personal responsibility. Every person on this earth should seek to make sure that they are walking in fullness of truth. This means dealing with all the issues we have addressed.

We need to be living a life of sacrifice and letting Jesus guide our lives, so that we are letting go of our ways of viewing life, theories, and fantasies. I believe as Christians, we should always challenge ourselves to go beyond the knowledge we have been taught. There is no urge to know more or to embrace other denominations, other people, and other ways. I believe this is also bondage as it can shipwreck our faith. We may never experience the fullness of God because of this.

It is our job that we are asking God to deliver us from these misconceptions, so that we really encounter the many things God has for us. We have only experienced a piece of God, but He wants us to experience Him in His fullness— to be His sons and daughters. The Bible says that the only desire that Father has is for us to be His sons and daughters - that is to be like Jesus (Ephesians 5:1).

It is our responsibility to pursue sanctification. He wants to remove our blemishes and everything that hinders us. It is only out of this that we can create a healthy church full of healthy individuals. Most of the time, we believe that it is the obligation of God to heal us, but it is up to us to seek deep healing and deliverance.

We can learn from Paul in 1 Corinthians 15:31 when he said "I die daily" that it is all about laying our lives down for Christ. He made a wilful choice to give his life for the sake of truth and intimacy with Him.

FOR REFLECTION:

1. What do you sense the Lord saying to you from this chapter?

_____

_____

_____

2. Write down 3 scriptures you feel may apply to this chapter:

_____

_____

_____

3. As you reflect on this chapter, what step will you take in your journey with Christ?

_____

_____

_____

CHAPTER 6

THE JOURNEY OF DISCOVERY

You must go on a journey of discovery. That means you must single-handedly come to God and ask yourself the question, "Who am I?" without the influences of religious propaganda, the world, parental influences, or friends! You need to go on a journey where you can find out who you truly are.

As you do that, you will unearth a lot of things about yourself. Knowing who you are creates a sense of stability which helps you to stay in path of truth. This will put you in a position where external influences will not derail you. It is of paramount importance to undertake this self-discovery journey so it can align your true identity and purpose on earth as God intended it.

Paul said in 1 Corinthians 9: 25 -26: All athletes are disciplined in their training. They do it to win a prize that will fade away, but we do it for an eternal prize. So, I run with purpose in every step. I am not just shadowboxing.

He meant that he needed to always check himself and stay on the right track so that when he preached, he would not fall short of what he was guiding others to do. How did he stay on that path of righteousness? He knew his identity and always operated from that place which his thoughts and behaviour were founded.

Many people fall into sin and lies because they do not know who they are. You are called on this earth to walk in a certain identity, and you must be careful to strip away all the false ones so that you are walking on the right path.

Many Christians are lost in the world through walking in half-truths, deception, or misinformation that we spoke about in previous chapters. Unfortunately, God is not the one really leading us. We need to strip away everything that deters us from walking on the right path.

FOR REFLECTION:

1. What do you sense the Lord saying to you from
   this chapter?

   _____

   _____

   _____

2. Write down 3 scriptures you feel may apply to this
   chapter:

   _____

   _____

   _____

3. As you reflect on this chapter, what step will you
   take in your journey with Christ?

   _____

   _____

   _____

CHAPTER 7

SEEKING INTIMACY

God was speaking to me about intimacy, and I heard Him say: "Intimacy is not only about coming to pray and having a routine. You must have a routine, yes, because I do like people who can plan for Me and be with Me and spend time with Me. However, how do you then become intimate with me? Being intimate with Me means that you engage Me in all that you do.

"It means that it does not matter where you are or what you are doing, you can always have Me around. Learn that skill to always engage and hear Me wherever you are, then you have now entered the realm of intimacy. I will work out that intimacy in your heart. I will build it up because you do not have the capacity to create intimacy on your own, thus, you have to come to Me".

The Bible says in Philippians 1:6, "And I am certain that God, who began the good work within you, will continue His work until it is finally finished on the day when Christ Jesus returns."

God is saying, "I am the one who does this work inside of you, but all I want is that you come to Me. What happens is that when you seek intimacy, it strengthens your identity and increases your knowledge of Me. It becomes something that is not just about the Bible or about prayer times – now it becomes more of a personal relationship. Like I said before, you are called to relationship then stewardship, but it is not about having mundane routines. It is Me being your friend— us doing things together. So, it becomes real, yet supernatural. That is what I am looking for; that is what I desire."

This means Jesus becomes part of our everyday life. Just like He said, "I only do what I see the Father do." (John 5:19). He was constantly communicating with the Father and was looking at what the Father was doing. For us to be imitators (Ephesians 5:1), we must grow into that place where we can see and hear God constantly. That way, we can truly grow into a place of intimacy, which helps us to be on the right track.

When we follow this path, we will no longer be bound by our cultures, environment, past or experiences. We can experience God for ourselves and no longer rely on other people to show us who God is. That way, we can get to stay on the straight and narrow path.

FOR REFLECTION:

1. What do you sense the Lord saying to you from this chapter?

_____

_____

_____

2. Write down 3 scriptures you feel may apply to this chapter:

_____

_____

_____

3. As you reflect on this chapter, what step will you take in your journey with Christ?

_____

_____

_____

CHAPTER 8

A PROPHETIC WORD:
TAKE UP YOUR SWORD!

Christians, take up your swords!
I just want to say that you must take up your sword and be strong in this time. There are many things that hold us back, and every day there are new things - new propagandas - whether from the government or the people around us. Many things can come in the way of our Christian walk, and I just want to encourage you that God just wants you. God wants you to do His work, and be in a deep relationship with you, that is all that really matters. In the end, God will only ask you about those two things.

In case sins keep pulling you backwards or you feel unfulfiled, I am asking God to help you in this time. I want you to take this advice and ask yourself, "What am I going to do next, and what am I going to do with my life? I really want to make an impact and a legacy." The only way to make an impact and legacy here on Earth is for us to really take up our swords. What I mean by that is: let us do this walk of intimacy and let us steward the things that God has given us. Those two things will lead us into our destiny, and destiny is particularly important.

If you can fulfil your destiny, then you have left your mark here on Earth and you will have crowns in Heaven. Heaven has crowns and Heaven has seats; it has seats of honour that are waiting for us and the only way to get to those things is by fulfiling our destiny. So, what is your destiny? This is a journey you must take. How are you going to seek the Father intimately? It is not just by knowing Him because you heard a sermon, or because it is in the Bible or it is recorded through to another person. It is really by placing the responsibility on yourself to seek Him wherever you are and in whatever you are doing.

The song, *Amazing Grace,* says that we were lost, but now, we are found. I believe that this is a continuous thing - we must be found all the time. That means we must always come into a place of truth because somewhere, sometimes, we do get lost in our cultures, thoughts or religious backgrounds. We do get lost in the things of this world; therefore, we must always come back to a place where we are found.

We need to keep asking God to help us. We need to continuously check that we are having that fulfilment that God promised us in the Word. He said that we will have abundance (John 10:10). That means we will have abundance in all things which is His presence, wealth, and everything that this earth has for us.

If we are not walking in that, then we must question why. There could be something potentially limiting our spirituality. We may be lost somewhere, and we need to find that fulfilment. We must all live an abundant life.

I believe that the keys given to you in this book, if you take them seriously with your whole heart, will help you to come into a place of abundance. Something will change and move. So, be encouraged at this time, take up your sword and be who you are meant to be!

FOR REFLECTION:

1. What do you sense the Lord saying to you from this chapter?

_____

_____

_____

2. Write down 3 scriptures you feel may apply to this chapter:

_____

_____

_____

3. As you reflect on this chapter, what step will you take in your journey with Christ?

_____

_____

_____

APPENDIX A:

RE-DISCOVERY PERSONAL PROFILE

There is absolutely nothing in this world more frustrating than not knowing or understand your identity, who you truly are and the purpose of your life. I truly believe that whether we like it or not, this question of purpose tends to have power over everything that surrounds our daily lives as it constructs us to act and behave accordingly. When we have no clear idea of who we truly are, we base who we should be on the image that society presents to us.

Consequently, we live our lives behind the identity of other people, imitating their identity, rather than spending the time to re-discover who we really are.
Hence why i have taking the time to put this profile together to help you re-discover, evaluate and recognise your authority, gifting and personal purpose.

God bless you.

1. WHAT IS MY DEEPEST DESIRE?
(Not what I have a general or passing "interest" in, but rather a deep yearning or aspiration to do.)

2. WHAT AM I TRULY PASSIONATE ABOUT?
(What do I really care about? What gifts and abilities do I especially enjoy using?)

3. WHAT MAKES ME ANGRY?
(Not destructive anger, which is selfishly motivated, but constructive anger that is based on compassion for others and a desire for people to be treated right, anger that is grieved by injustices and that leads to positive action to remedy problems.)

4. WHAT IDEAS ARE PERSISTENT IN MY HEART AND THOUGHTS?
(What recurring dreams do I have for my life? What idea never leaves me?)

5. WHAT DO I CONSTANTLY IMAGINE MYSELF DOING?
(What do I dream about becoming? What gifts or skills would I use and develop to become this?)

6. WHAT DO I WANT TO DO FOR HUMANITY?
(What kind of impact would I like to have on my community? What do I want to pass along to the next generation? What would I like to be remembered for?)

7. WHAT WOULD BRING ME THE GREATEST FULFILLMENT?

(What three endeavours or achievements have given me the greatest satisfaction and fulfilment in life so far, and why? What motivates and gratifies me the most, and how can I incorporate it into my life as my vocation or life focus?)

8. WHAT WOULD I DO FOR NO MONEY OR OTHER COMPENSATION?

(What activities am I currently receiving satisfaction from that I am not being paid for? What am I so dedicated to that I would continue to do it even if I stopped receiving money for it? What would I do for no compensation?

9. WHAT WOULD I RATHER BE DOING?

(What do I wish I were doing when I am doing other things? What makes me feel most at home when I am doing it?

10. WHAT WOULD I DO IF I KNEW I COULD NOT FAIL?

(What endeavour, enterprise, creative work, project, or plan would I engage in if it were risk-free? If money were no object? If I did not worry that I had the wrong background, the wrong looks, the wrong job experiences, or the wrong anything else?)

11. WHAT IS THE MOST IMPORTANT THING I COULD DO WITH MY LIFE?

(Above all other things, what is the most significant thing I could do with my life? What do I want to occur in my

life? How do I want to live my life based on my values and beliefs?)

12. WHAT ENDEAVOR OR ACTIVITY WOULD BEST CONNECT ME TO MY CREATOR?

(What draws me closest to God?)

APPENDIX B:

PERSONAL SUMMARY STATEMENT:

WHAT I BELIEVE I WAS PUT ON THIS EARTH TO DO

Documenting your personal purpose and gift: *In what specific ways have I exercised this gift in the past? How can I build on this in the future?*

Exercising and refining your personal gift: *In what ways will I develop and apply my personal gift now that I know what it is?*

Releasing your personal gift: Who *has the knowledge, skills, and commitment to help me to release my gift?*

CONTACT

For further information please contact **Claver** on:
Tel: **07562 203 735**
Email: **purposeofexistence@hotmail.com**

Reviews

The compelling fact of Claver Lukoki's life is that he carries a burning passion to impact, envision and influence his generation to rise to their God intended purpose and to make a difference in their own lives and their generation. His book contains great revelation knowledge. If you are not sure of your life's worth and purpose, I highly recommend this book to you.
— *Bishop Abel Kungu Snr.*

Getting a head start with Claver has been hugely beneficial and I'm learning more about myself as well everyday.
— *Janeil*

I used to think that you had to be an adult to discover your purpose but now I know it can be done at any age with the help of the Lord.
— *Abel kungu Jnr*

I always thought that purpose was for adults and I'm just a kid, so I'm not supposed to think about any of that. I am so blessed to have Claver in my life because without him I would not have discovered my purpose or had this opportunity, so thank you.
This is just the beginning of my life.
— *Tiaara Mpanumpanu*

Purpose. Something I had but didn't see. Something I longed for but didn't allow. Claver not only took his time to help me understand the purpose of my existence but many others alongside me. God has a plan for me and with his guidance and the guidance of many more my purpose remains an open door .

— *Anesu*

NOTE

Printed in Great Britain
by Amazon

10019466R00045